The Quotes within this book
aim to help the reader
cope with Discrimination.

"WHEN YOU LOOK AT ME WHAT DO YOU SEE? IS IT WHAT YOU WOULD HAVE ME BE OR DO YOU SEE ME?"

LUCIA PARAVIA

FOCUS ON YOUR
INNER STRENGTH
RATHER THAN ON
HOW OTHERS MAKE
YOU FEEL.

IT WASN'T MEANT
TO BE THIS WAY,
WORK THROUGH
EVERY CHALLENGE
UNDERSTANDING
YOU LEAVE A PATH
FOR THE NEXT
GENERATION.

JUST KNOW YOU
ARE FINE JUST
HOW YOU ARE.
DONT CHANGE TO
PLEASE OTHERS ,YOU
RISK YOUR UNIQUE
QUALITIES.

MANY SOLUTIONS
LIE WITHIN EVERY
HEART , LOOK
WITHIN AND LESS
OUTWARDS.

AT TIMES
DISCRIMINATION
LEADS PEOPLE TO
DARKNESS, YOU
MUST REMAIN TRUE
TO WHO YOU ARE
NOW AND WHO YOU
WOULD LIKE TO BE.
ALWAYS STAY IN
THE LIGHT.

LIKE THE RAGING
SEAS YOU ARE
UNABLE TO SWIM IN,
KNOW THE
ENVIRONMENT
WHERE TO WALK
AND BE EQUIPPED
WITH PATIENCE
AND WISDOM.

LETTING GO OF
HURTFUL REMARKS
THROUGH THE
GRACE OF
FORGIVENESS IS A
GIFT TO YOURSELF.

GO FORWARD WITH
YOUR HEAD UP,
NEVER FEAR.

FACE THE MORNING
WITH JOY, LOVE AND
HOPE. STRIVING
FOR PEACE. THE
BATTLE HAS BEEN
WON AND AINT
NOONE TAKING
THAT FROM YOU.

AT TIMES IT MAY
SEEM SO
IMPOSSIBLE WITH
THE BARRIERS
INFRONT OF YOU....
JUST KEEP PUSHING
FORWARD AND
DONT GIVE UP.

YOU ARE WORTHY,
WHATEVER YOU CAN
OR CAN'T DO ITS
OKAY. THE
CHALLENGE
DEVELOPS INTO AN
OPPORTUNITY FOR
GROWTH &
LEARNING.

THE WIND IN MY
BREATH , GOD
BREATHED INTO
ME, SHALL SPEAK
ONLY WORDS OF
UNITY.

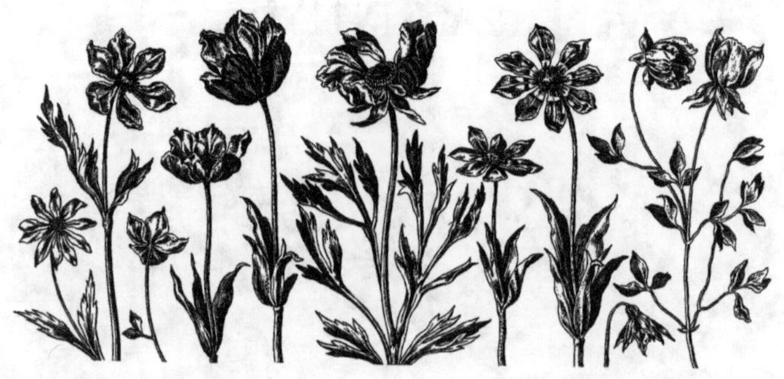

THE WORLD IS A
TEMPORARY PLACE,
LEAVE A HERO
FOOTPRINT TO
BETTER HUMANITY
AND THE WORLD.

ALTHOUGH YOUR
JUDGEMENT PIERCES
MY BEING , I WILL
SURVIVE.
MY LIGHT
SURROUNDS ME ,
MAY YOUR LIGHT
SURROUND YOU.

IN THE FACE OF
ADVERSITY WE
FIND OUR
STRENGTH IN THE
SHADOW OF
DISCRIMINATION
OUR UNITY SHINES
THE BRIGHTEST.

THIS IS YOUR LIFE, DO EVERYTHING YOU LIKE TO, DONT WAIT FOR CONFIRMATION FROM ANYONE. BELIEVE IN YOU !

THE JOURNEY
THROUGH
DISCRIMINATION IS
A TESTAMENT TO
OUR RESILENCE.
TURNING SCARS
INTO STORIES OF
TRIUMPH.

AGAINST THE
BACKDROP OF
DISCRIMINATION
OUR SPIRITS RISE
AS A BEACON OF
HOPE FORGING A
PATH TO EQUALITY.

AS WE WEATHER
DISCRIMINANTION'S
STORM, REMEMBER
EVERY CHALLENGE
IS AN OPPORUNITY
TO REWRITE
HISTORY.

IF I HAD A COIN
FOR EVERY TEAR I
HAVE SHED I
WOULD BE A
BILLIOAIRE.
SAVE THE TEARS.

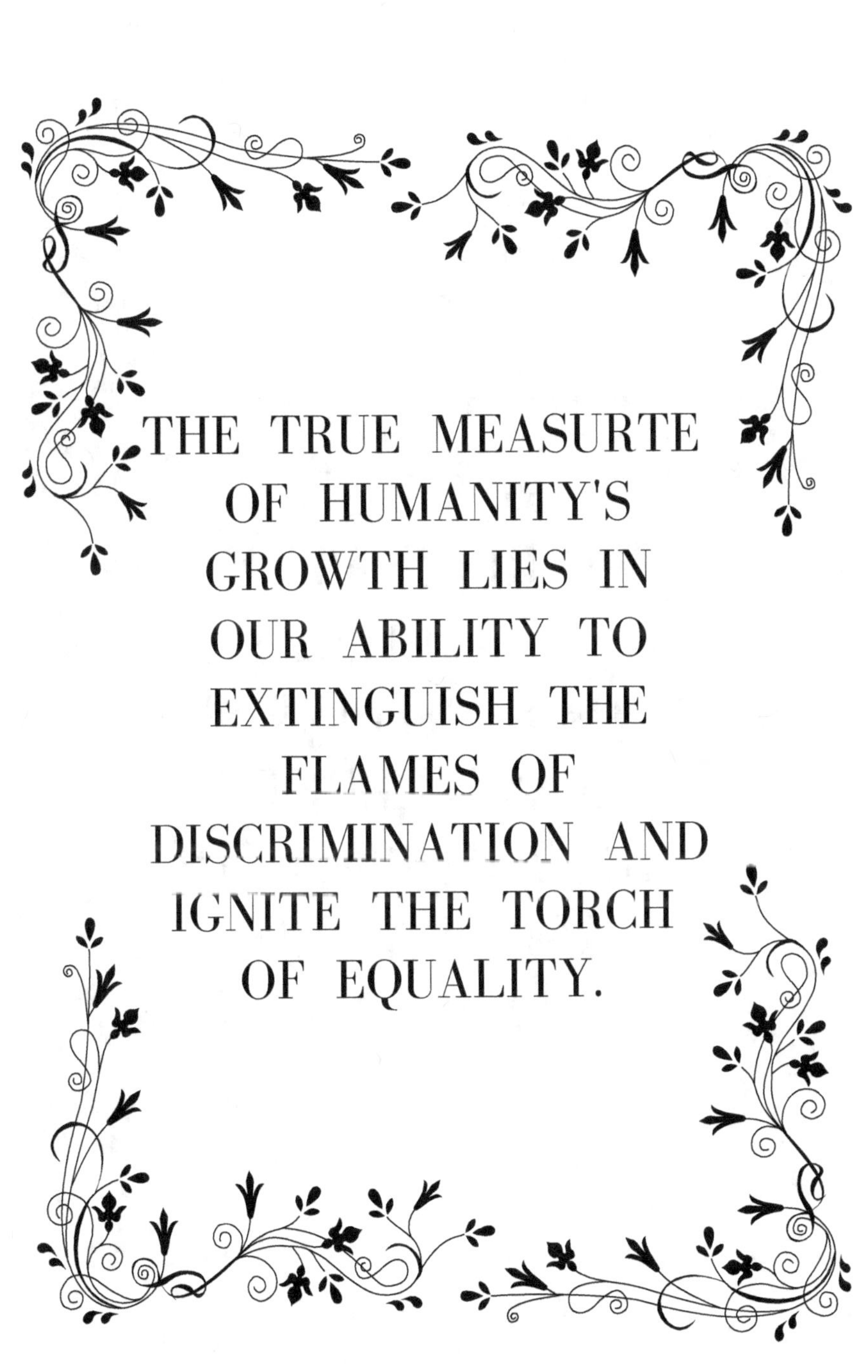
THE TRUE MEASURTE
OF HUMANITY'S
GROWTH LIES IN
OUR ABILITY TO
EXTINGUISH THE
FLAMES OF
DISCRIMINATION AND
IGNITE THE TORCH
OF EQUALITY.

THE BATTLE
AGAINST
DISCRIMINATION
SHOULD BE
CONFRONTED WITH
KNOWLEDGE
AND EMPATHY AS
THE SHIELD.

THE ESSENCE OF
YOU WILL OVERRIDE
EVERY PAINFUL
ENCOUNTER OF
DISCRIMINATION.

WHAT IS YOUR
WEAKNESS COULD
BECOME YOUR
STRENGTH.

WHO WOULD YOU BE
WITHOUT
DISCRIMINATION ?
BE THAT PERSON.

THE SONG OF A
BIRD,
THE BRIGHT SUNNY
MORNING,
THE STARRY NIGHT,
THE WHISPER OF A
OLD OAK TREE,
BRINGS FORWARD
PEACE TO YOU.
HOLD IT IN YOUR
HEART, & SPIRIT
FOR A LIFETIME.

LOVE AT ALL
TIMES.
HATE HAS NO
PLACE IN YOUR
LIFE.

SOME DAYS ARE
BETTER TO WAIT
FOR THE SUN TO
GO DOWN AND
RISE IN THE
MORNING.

HERE FOR BUT A MOMENT IN TIME, JUST PASSING THROUGH, HOLD UNTO YOUR TREASURES FOREVER.

THE STARE THAT
STINGS ,
THE LAUGH THAT
MOCKS , IS FIRE.
BE A VESSEL OF
WATER.

THE THORN THAT
STOLE MY DESTINY
HAS BEEN
OVERRIDED TODAY.

I AM BEAUTIFUL,
I AM WHO I AM
MEANT TO BE,
JUST AS MY MAKER
INTENDED FOR ME.

LOVE WILL SUSTAIN
YOU THROUGH
DESPAIR.

THE LONG
DIFFICULT JOURNEY
OF DISCRIMINATION
BRINGS YOU TO A
COMPLETE JOURNEY
OF LIFE.

I SEE IT IN MY GRASP, A PLACE OF FREEDOM

IT IS IMPOSSIBLE
TO PLEASE EVERY
HUMAN IN THIS
WORLD,
STAY WITH WHO
YOU PLEASE.

HUMANS WILL
ALWAYS JUDGE,
YOU CHOOSE TO
LISTEN OR WALK
AWAY

HOW HARD THE
WORLD MAY TRY
TO DIMINISH YOUR
LIGHT, BUT YOU
ARE MORE
SUPERNATURAL
THAN YOU KNOW.
SHINE BRIGHT !

HURTFUL INJUSTICE
HAS NO HOLD ON
YOU, YOU ARE IN
CONTROL.

LET YOUR
DETERMINATION
AND COURAGE BE
THE LIGHT THAT
GUIDES YOU
THROUGH THE
DARKNESS OF
DISCRIMINATION.

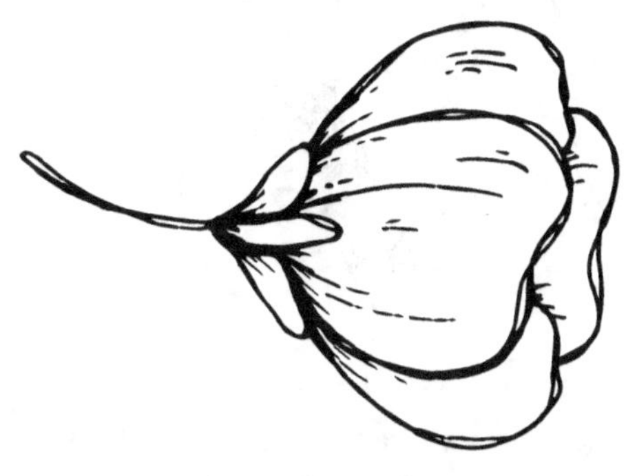

OPEN YOURSELF
ONLY TO GOOD,
CLOSE THE DOOR
TO
DISCRIMINATION.

LOOK WITHIN A
PLACE IN YOUR
HEART
TO FIND THE
KNOWLEDGE FOR
UNITY.

I KNOW THERE
WILL BE A TIME
THAT I WILL FEEL
THE SENSE OF
TOTAL LOVELINESS.

COPING WITH
DISCRIMINATION
REQUIRES A
STEADFAST HEART.

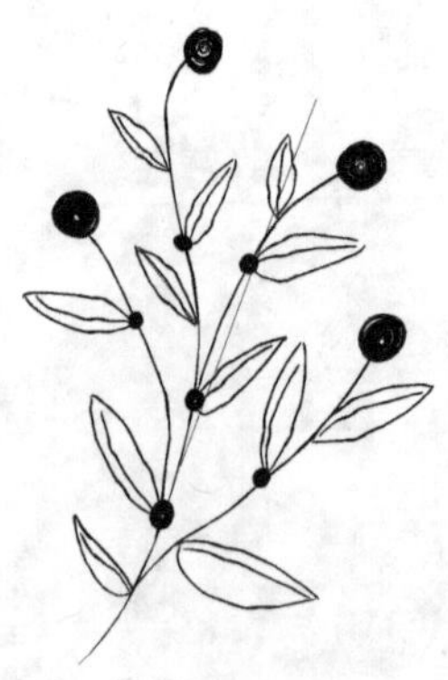

THERE WILL BE A
MOMENT IN TIME
THAT WILL
EXTEND, WHERE
ALL THE PIECES
WILL FIT INTO
PLACE..

WHEN YOU FEEL
LIKE HUMANS ARE
SQUEEZING YOU
OUT OF YOUR OWN
EXISTENCE REMAIN
FIRM.

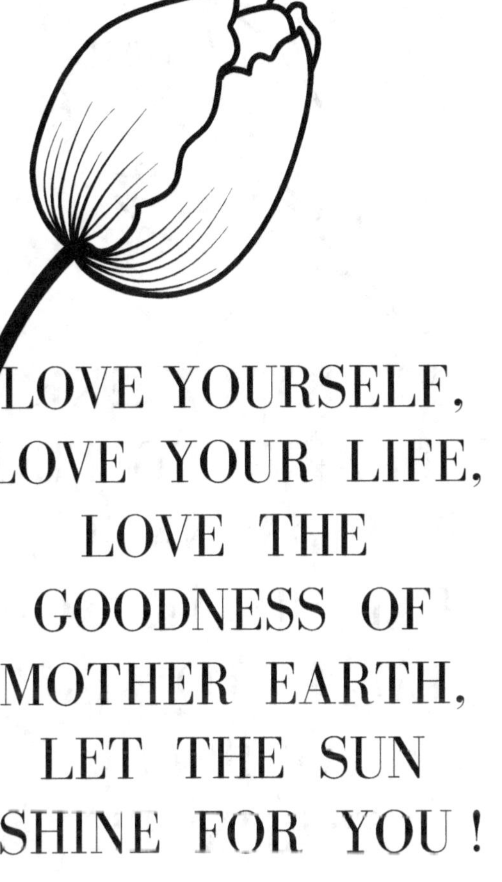
LOVE YOURSELF,
LOVE YOUR LIFE,
LOVE THE
GOODNESS OF
MOTHER EARTH,
LET THE SUN
SHINE FOR YOU !

EVERY STRIKE
EXPEREINCED FROM
DISCRIMINATION
MAY BREAK YOU,
FLIP IT TO MAKE
YOURSELF
STRONGER.

THE LONGING IN
MY HEART WILL
BE CONNECTED TO
MY MAKER FIXING
EVERY INCH OF
ME.

BE KIND TO YOURSELF , SHOW KINDNESS TO OTHERS.

IN THE JOURNEY OF
LIFE
DISCRIMINATION IS
A HURDLE NOT A
DESTINATION.

USE THE MOST POWERFUL TOOLS SUCH AS SELF-LOVE AND SELF-BELIEF IN WINNING THE BATTLE OF DISCRIMINATION.

DEVELOP THE KNOWLEDGE TO GUIDE YOU THROUGH TOUGH TIMES AND NEVER DOUBT YOURSELF.

LOVE YOURSELF
MORE THAN YOU
LOVE THE WORLD.

LET YOUR ANGER
PUSH YOU TO DO
GOOD.

DISCRIMINATION IS
LIKE MOULD,
YOU NEED TO
CONSTANTLY
CLEAN IT UP.

DISCRIMINATION IS A REFLECTION OF OTHERS IGNORANCE.

DONT LET THE
NEGATIVITY OF
DISCRIMINATION
DEFINE WHO YOU
ARE.

DONT SHY AWAY FROM DISCRIMINATION, STAND UP AND KNOW YOUR RIGHTS.

FEELING LIKE A
MISFIT SHOULD
NOT LAST A
LIFETIME,
LIVE WHERE YOU
ARE APPRECIATED
AND CAN MAKE A
POSITIVE
DIFFERENCE.

SOME DAYS ARE
BETTER ALONE,
ENJOYING YOUR
OWN COMPANY.

EVERY POSITIVE
ACTION AGAINST
DISCRIMINATION
SETS A STANDARD
FOR A MORE
INCLUSIVE WORLD.

TRIUMPHING OVER
ADVERSITY MAY
REQUIRE PRACTICE.

YOU COULD SPEND
EVERY MINUTE OF
EVERYDAY ASKING
WHY OR YOU
COULD SPEND
YOUR TIME DOING
WHAT YOU LOVE.

LIVING IN THIS
COMPLICATED
WORLD IS
SUFFICIENT, NOONE
DESERVES TO BE
DISCRIMINATED
AGAINST.

WHAT GETS TAKEN
FROM A HUMAN
DEALING WITH
DISCRIMINATION
CAN BE RETRIEVED
BUT THE HUMAN
DISCRIMINATING
HAS LOST
SOMETHING
FOREVER.

YOU ARE HERE
FOR A VERY
SPECIAL REASON.
DONT LET OTHERS
SPOIL THAT.

IN OUR
DIFFERENCES WE
FIND COMMMON
GROUND TO UNITE
AND CREATE
HARMONY IN THIS
WORLD.

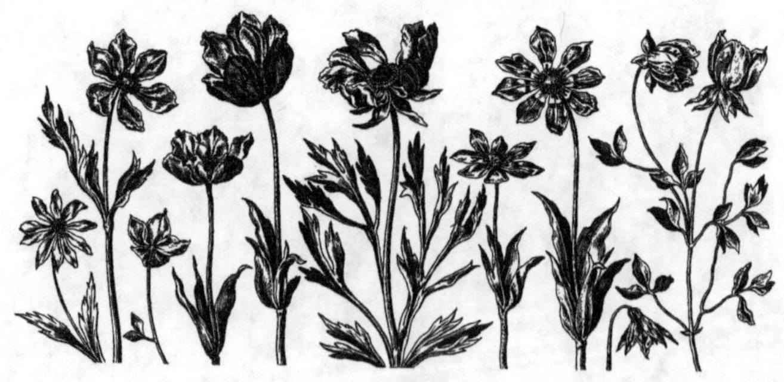

GOOD HUMANS
RESPECT OTHERS
DIFFERENCES ,
REMAIN CLOSE TO
THEM.

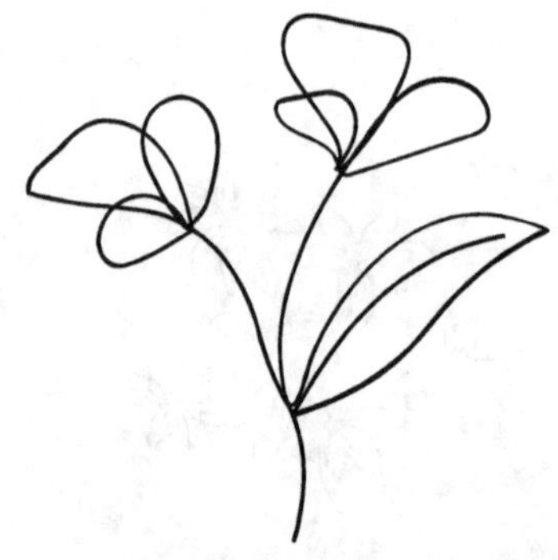

LOVE LIFE,
EVERY SECOND,
EVERY MINUTE,
EVERY HOUR,
EVERYDAY
FOR
A
LIFETIME.

KNOW THERE IS
ALWAYS SOMEONE
DOING IT MORE
DIFFCULT THAN
YOU AND OTHERS
BETTER .
BE GRATEFUL.

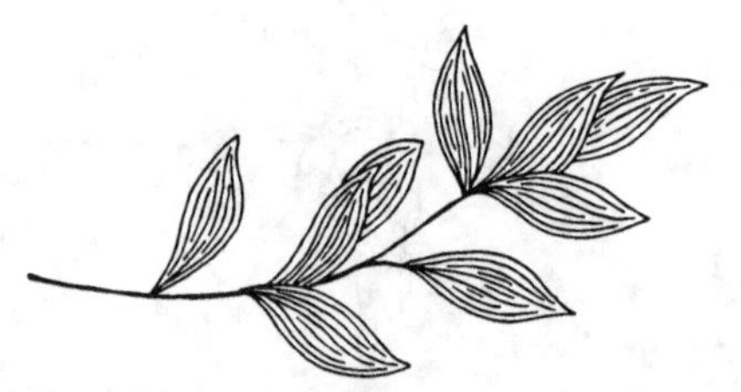

WHEN ALL ELSE
FAILS LOOK AT
THE BLUE SKY,
FEEL THE WIND IN
YOUR FACE, THE
WARMTH OF THE
SUN AND THE
FEELING OF HOPE
FOR A BRIGHTER
NEXT DAY.

I HAD A VISION OF GOOD

I STARTED ON THE ROAD
WITH FIRE IN MY SOUL,
WITH THE GRACE OF GOD WITHIN
ME, ALTHOUGH AMONGST MY
JOURNEY I ENCOUNTERED FATIGUE,
SELF DOUBT, HOW MUCH HARDER DO
I HAVE TO GIVE, PUSH LIKE NEVER
BEFORE CHRIST IN MY BONES
MISSION FOR GOOD I AM HALF WAY
THERE,
HOLD ON , PUSH ON, AND DONT STOP
THE VOICE OF MERCY RINGING IN
MY EARS , MY SWEET MAKER I
REJOICE KNOWING YOU REMAIN
FOREVER, CAN'T SEE THE WAY, FEEL
SO LOST BACK AND FORWARD , I GO
WITH YOUR WAY , YOUR NAME,
I SEE IT,
IT'S IN MY GRASP , I HEAR YOU GOD,
SAYING TAKE IT , HAVE NO FEAR, MY
LOVE ABUNDANCE AND SUFFICIENT
GRACE,
MY LOVING FATHER,
I REACHED MY CAPACITY, I REACHED
MY DESTINATION , NOW ITS YOU , ALL
YOU GOD , MERCIFUL GOD HAVE
GRACE UPON ME,
I AM TO WORSHIP , SHOW GRATITUDE,
THERE IS NO OTHER PLACE TO BE ,
IT IS HERE, IN THE PRESENCE OF
YOUR MIGHTY POWER TO GUIDE ME
THROUGH DISCRIMINATION.